The Instant Pot Soup Cookbook

Best Soup Recipes for Your Electric Pressure Cooker

Nelly Grant

PUBLISHED BY:

Nelly Grant

Copyright © 2017 All rights reserved

All rights reserved. No part of this Book may be reproduced or transmitted in any form or by any means, electronic or mechanical, including photocopying, recording or by any information storage and retrieval system, without written permission from the author.

Disclaimer

The recipes and information in this book are provided for educational purposes only. Please always consult a licensed professional before making changes to your lifestyle or diet. The author and publisher shall have neither liability nor responsibility to anyone concerning any loss or damage caused or alleged to be caused directly or indirectly by the information contained in this book. All trademarks and brands within this book are for clarifying purposes only and are owned by the owners themselves, not affiliated with this document.

Your Gift!

We want to show our appreciation that you support our work,

so we have put together a gift for you.

Just visit the link on the last page of this book to download it now.

We now You will love this gift.

Thanks!

Table of Contents

Introduction	6
Chapter 1: How To Properly And Safely Use The Instant Pot	7
The Buttons	7
Things You Need To Know About the Instant Pot	10
Pressure Release	12
Opening the Instant Pot	13
Chapter 2: Instant Pot FAQ	14
Chapter 3: Benefits of Instant Pot	16
Intelligent Programming	17
Automatic Cooking	18
Eliminating Harmful Micro-Organisms in Food	19
Chapter 4: Soup Recipes	21
Carrot Pork Soup	21
Italian Chicken Sausage Soup	23
Minestrone Soup	25
Chicken Lentil Soup	27
Kale Soup	29
Beef Quinoa Soup	31
Turkey Mixed Bean Soup	33
Pepe Beef Soup	35
Bacon Spinach Soup	37
Mango Dal	39
Chicken Tortilla Soup	41
Pea Lentil Soup	43
Broccoli Cheddar Soup	45
Tomato Soup	47

Chicken Noodle Soup	49
Baked Potato Soup	51
Minestrone Soup	53
Turkey Noodle Soup	55
Cauliflower Potato Soup	57
Easy Cream of Broccoli Soup	59
Chapter 5. Vegetarian Soup Recipes	61
Butternut Squash Curry Soup	61
Pure Black Beans Soup	63
Mushroom Milk Soup	65
Baby Potato Soup	67
Sweet Potatoes, Kale and Yellow Split-Pea Soup	69
Spicy Vegetable Soup	71
Veggie-Quinoa Soup	73
Chipotle Pumpkin Soup	75
Mexican Baked Potato Soup	77
Lentil Red Curry & Coconut Milk Soup	79
Taco Soup	81
Sweet Potato and Red Curry Soup	83
Sweet Potato and Peanut Butter Soup	85
Cabbage Leek Diet Soup	87
Curried Butternut Squash Soup	89
Spicy Collards and Black-eyed Pea Soup	91
Collard Greens and White Bean Soup	93
Green Moong Dal / Green Gram Lentil Soup	95
Your Gift!	98

Introduction

The instant pot is an excellent kitchen appliance. It may seem a little one dimensional, but it is a great device for so many things. It can make yogurt or cook rice. The instant pot can be a slow cooker, a pressure cooker, and also an oven for baking!

This Instant Pot Cookbook will give you access to some of the easiest and most delicious Soup recipes to use with your instant pot. The instant pot is good for experienced cooks as well as beginners.

Living busy doesn't mean that you should be obliged to eat food that isn't delicious and isn't healthy. This cookbook presents you a better choice. Only add the ingredients, set the timer, and in 30 minutes or less, you will have a nice meal worth enjoying. The Instant Pot doesn't need hours of time to prepare or to plan.

So, flip through the pages and decide what you are making for dinner!

Chapter 1: How To Properly And Safely Use The Instant Pot

Often, when one gets an Instant pot, they don't know what to do with it. There are so many buttons there, and the first thing you should learn is how you can use the instant pot. There are also some frequently-asked-questions in the next chapter to help you use your Instant Pot Effectively.

The Buttons

You've probably noticed that your instant pot has a ton of buttons. It seems like a lot, but there are various uses for this. This section will go over the buttons you use the most.

- **Sauté:** this is the one that you can use to brown your food, but along with that, you can use it to help cook and thicken stews and soups. You should use this with the lid off, and you can adjust it to more or less to a simmer.

- **Keep warm/cancel:** this does what it says it does. You can either keep food warm or cancel it. Typically, the temperature for keeping it warm is about 145 but can be adjusted.

- **Manual:** this is to cook anything on high pressure for a certain time. You can adjust the time as needed.

There are specific buttons as well that are important to know about when using the instant pot, and they are listed as follows:

- **Soup:** this does it on high pressure for 30 minutes.

- **Meat/Stew:** this cooks it on high pressure for 35 minutes.

- **Bean/Chili:** this adjusts the pressure to 30 minutes on high.

- **Poultry:** When you use this setting, it is important for you to know that it is only to be used for small portions of poultry because it will only cook on high pressure for 15 minutes. You can adjust the timer.

- **Rice:** this cooks on low pressure automatically. This is great for cooking rice, and you can adjust based on the water.

- **Multigrain:** this will cook on high pressure for 40 minutes.

- **Porridge:** this will cook it on high pressure for about 20 minutes.

- **Steam:** this will cook it on high pressure for 10 minutes. In this function, you should have the steamer basket there, and it will be at full power the entire time, which means you don't want the food to be directly at the bottom. Often, once it reaches the highest pressure, it'll cycle the pressure again.

- **Slow cooker:** this will cook it for 4 hours automatically. You can do it on low, which is around 190-201 degrees, normal which go from 194-205, and high which goes from 199-210.

- **Pressure:** you can switch between high and low pressure.

- **Yogurt:** this is used for making yogurt in separate jars.

- **Timer:** this is for delayed cooking. To use this, choose a function, make adjustments, and then adjust with the plus and minus buttons.

All of these specific functions can be changed with the plus and minus buttons, changing the default cooking time, so it cooks the food effectively.

You should try to consider ones that typically have the manual setting so that you can adjust the time. When you're ready, you can move to more specific ones, allowing you to create more food.

Things You Need To Know About the Instant Pot

While we've gone over the functions of it, there are a few things that you should know about the instant pot, and they are listed here in this section.

The first is that it's easy to clean. You won't spend lots of time with so many different appliances, but the instant pot will also save your kitchen space. If you've had a slow cooker, pressure cooker, a rice cooker, and so many other tools, replaces it with the instant pot, and it'll save your room.

Another important thing to know is that the instant pot typically runs at 11.6 psi, which is around 242 degrees. Other pressure cookers are usually around 15 psi. when you're using a recipe that's used in your typical pressure cooker, make sure that you do accommodate a few extra minutes in the Instant Pot.

Another important element is that many people assume you can pressure can in your instant pot. The answer to that is that's not the case. Because it's regulated by a pressure sort of sensor instead of the temperature, the temperature of the IP depends on location. It's not been tested for pressure canning, and it's best not to use it for that.

One thing that you should get as well is a second stainless steel insert. You might already have one with your instant pot, but it's great to have in case your first one is in the dishwasher. Not only that, if you're bulk cooking for the week, and you want to create a couple of different dinners, having multiples of these is good so that you do not have to spend extra time cleaning it. It's a great extra item to have around and won't take up space.

Another great thing is that you can create so many different dinners with this. There are a lot of things that you can make. For example, consider the following:

1. Skillet dinners can be made in 5-8 minutes, including pasta and various veggies and meats. Simply brown the veggies, and then toss it in.
2. Beans are another great thing to help if you're looking for a low-calorie and high protein dish. Dry beans can be made in about 8-9 minutes, and you can even make a pot of chili in an instant pot.
3. Yogurt can also be made here. It only quires one appliance, some time, and a good eye, but it's worth it for it'll save you money.

4. Rice is also another one. You can use the rice function, allowing it to come out as a perfect dish.
5. Steamed foods: the steaming function is often one of the best parts of this. You'll be able to keep the vitamins and minerals in there without the calories, and you'll be able to do it with a trivet in your instant pot and water in the bottom, making some great dishes

These quick little tidbits do show the power of the instant pot, and it's something that can certainly help you in your journey to create the best and most satisfying instant pot dishes.

Pressure Release

One thing you'll notice in your instant pot recipes is that it says the words "quick release" and "natural pressure release".

The first is to understand that **quick release** will release the inner pressure of this immediately. This will stop your cooking process to prevent overcooking any food. If you're cooking veggies quickly, or seafood that is delicate and shouldn't be cooked too much, then quick release is what you want.

The second function is the **natural release** or natural pressure release. This will release the pressure and steam in gradual increments. This is good for food with a lot of foam, lots of liquid, or a lot of starch in it. For many who use it, if you're using a lot of cooking meat, this is the way to go, since it won't affect the overall flavor of the food

A good thing to notice is that if you're using a thicker liquid, you might notice that there is less steam. If you notice this, it might start to cause the instant pot not to reach the pressure cooking cycle, do consider adding either chicken stock or water to this. If you see that it needs to be thickened, it's best to put this all in the instant pot once you cook it, so that it's not affecting the cooking process.

Opening the Instant Pot

Opening the instant pot is very important since there is a load of pressure there which can cause it to hurt you potentially. This section will go over how to open an instant pot effectively

The first is to make sure that the pressure is released completely before you open this. You'll see the floating valve, and when it's gone, it'll drop. If you want to make it go faster, turn the venting knob to the venting area to make sure that all the pressure is gone.

When opening it, tilt it away from you. You should use the lid as a guide to keep the steam away from you. The lid will shield you in case if something happens so that you don't get hurt.

If you have the sealing ring already there, make sure that it's taken off so that you can pop it. After that, it's pretty easy, and you can then, after the heat is initially released, take the contents out.

Chapter 2: Instant Pot FAQ

Find a list of the typical questions asked about the instant pot to help you understand before you use this.

1. **Do you use the chicken button or the manual button for chicken?**

It depends. If your recipe calls for one, use it. If you're doing a whole huge chicken, it's best to use the manual setting. To get a more particular flavor, try the poultry settings

2. **Are there any directions on how to use the manual function?**

The manual function does exactly what it says, and it'll cook it naturally for the desired time. Just set the time, and then press it, and it'll cook it once it's totally built up.

3. **The pot isn't' heating up on manual, what's going on?**

Manual adjusts the cooking time. However, if the contents are frozen, you'll start to notice that the countdown will only happen when the pressure is reached. Also, take a look at the liquid you have in there as well, it might cause the pressure to be lacking.

4. How long does it take to warm up before cooking?

Usually about 5-7 minutes. Use the warm liquid to help bring the pressure up faster.

5. Do you need to do an initial test run?

It's recommended, simply because you'll understand how to use this better. Often, people don't understand, so try using the water to test how fast it heats up before it cooks.

6. How do you get low -pressure?

It's simple. There is a pressure button, and first, you can press manual, and then press the pressure button until its low. You can then press the timer buttons to adjust the time

7. Can you change the heat on sauté mod?

You sure can. You press the adjust button, and then choose the three levels of temperature. Most people use it on normal, but occasionally, if you want to boil something, put it on more.

Chapter 3: Benefits of Instant Pot

Pressure-cooking has several advantages like saving time and energy, preserving the nutrients in the food and eliminating all the harmful microorganisms that might be present in the food. Let us take a look at all the different benefits of cooking in an Instant Pot.

Saving Time & Energy

Food can be cooked much faster by pressure-cooking than by any other method of cooking. An Instant Pot can help you in reducing the time of your cooking by 70% when compared to the other methods of cooking. Since much less water is made use of in cooking and it is cooked in a fully insulated pot, much less energy is required as well when compared to any other cooking technique like boiling or steaming while cooking on a stove top. An Instant Pot will help you in saving energy when compared to microwave.

Preserving Nutrients & Cook Tasty Food

Pressure-cooking will help in ensuring that the heat is spread evenly and quickly. You don't have to immerse your food in the water, but there needs to be sufficient water to ensure that there is steam in the Pot and that it is sufficient. Because of this, all the nutrients in the food, like the different minerals and vitamins will stay intact in the food and won't dissipate. Steam will surround the food so that it won't become oxidized by air or exposure to heat. Therefore, fresh green foods will retain their color even after being cooked.

An Instant Pot has a unique cooking mechanism where the food stays fully sealed. No steam or any smells will spread throughout your home or your kitchen. This makes for a clean and extremely convenient cooking experience. Instant Pot tends to take advantage of different techniques for cooking flavorful meals that retain all their nutrients. Due to the cooking cycles that are controlled by microprocessors, all the meals are cooked consistently.

The food that is cooked in Instant Pot is cooked in a fully sealed container. This means that all the nutrients and flavors in the ingredients are trapped within the container. The water content and the fresh juices within all the ingredients will stay in the Instant Pot and won't dissipate. While you are steaming food in Instant Pot, you needn't make use of lots of water. You need to add enough water to keep the cooker filled with pressure. This makes sure that all the vitamins and minerals within the food don't escape and aren't dissolved because of water. Pressure-cooking also allows whole grains and beans based meals to have a softer texture and they will taste much better as well.

Another important feature of this appliance is that all the meals will be cooked consistently. This is possible because of the intelligent programming that makes sure that similar foods are cooked in a similar manner and also due to the even distribution of heat while cooking.

Intelligent Programming

The Instant Pot has 12 operation buttons that will perform different cooking tasks like cooking rice, multigrain rice, sautéing, soup, poultry, meat and stew, chili and beans, steaming, slow cooking, keeping warm and even for making yogurt. These one-button functions will help you in achieving consistent results. For instance, take the "rice" button. While cooking rice, the Instant Pot will estimate the required amount of rice and water by measuring out the pre-heating time. The duration of the pressure keeping will vary depending upon this measurement and the stage of cooking. Each of these function buttons can be refined further by varying the range of the food from rare to well done, depending on your preferences.

Automatic Cooking

This is convenient and is an automated process. Each cook can be time and then it would simply switch onto keeping the food warm once it is cooked. Unlike a conventional pressure cooker, you needn't stand and monitor the cooking time and process. Delayed Cooking is another fetching feature of the Instant Pot. This means that you can plan your meal well ahead of time. You needn't stand around and wait for your meal to be ready. This means that more than half reduces your cooking time. Wouldn't it be wonderful if you can come home to a freshly cooked meal and you don't have to worry about doing a lot of dishes once you are done with the meal?

The Instant Pot is energy efficient, and it saves up to 70% of energy when compared to other appliances like stove, steamer and so on.

Conventional cookers have an image of these spitting and steaming monstrous pots that keep making rattling noises that can even scare an adult. The Instant Pot is quite the opposite of this. The Instant Pot is quiet and is fully sealed. This means that the pressure simply builds up in the inner pot and there is no chance of any steam escaping into the outer environment. Therefore, there won't be any smell spreading in your home or kitchen. Like mentioned earlier, this will help in trapping the flavors of the food within the container. Instant Pot will help you in cooking food without heating up the surroundings, and this would be well appreciated during summer time by reducing the electricity required for heating and cooling the food. The Instant Pot does help you in keeping your kitchen clean. There won't be any messy spills or splashes, and you don't have to clean up food that boils over. Everything is perfectly sealed and trapped within the inner pot. It is a kitchen-friendly appliance that requires minimal cleaning. It is a multipurpose appliance, and it will help you in getting rid of the clutter in your kitchen.

Eliminating Harmful Micro-Organisms in Food

When you prepare food at a temperature that is above the boiling point of water, and then this will help in killing all the harmful microorganisms that might be present in the ingredients like bacteria and viruses. Pressure-cooking is a good way to sterilize your food. Rice, wheat, corn and even beans tend to carry different fungal poisons referred to as aflatoxins. Different species of fungi produce these aflatoxins due to humid conditions and improper storage. Also, these are responsible for triggering a range of potent illnesses like liver cancer and might also play a role in hosting other triggers of cancer. Just heating the food to the boiling point of water does not necessarily destroy these harmful toxins. Cooking at that temperature helps. Kidney beans are a very common ingredient and are mostly made use of for cooking chili. Well, these kidney beans have a particular toxin that's present in them, and the only way in which this can be destroyed is by cooking them at a high temperature for at least of ten minutes.

Chapter 4: Soup Recipes

Carrot Pork Soup

Ingredients

- 24 ounces (680g) carrots
- 28 ounces (800 g) green radish
- 24 ounces (680g) pork shank
- 1 gal (4 L) water
- 1 inch (2.5cm) ginger
- 2 dried jujubes
- 1 small piece of chenpi
- Sea salt (as needed)

Preparation Method

1. Clean the Pork Shank; boil 2 quarts of water. Then, cook the pork shank for 3 minutes to clean and remove the excess fat. Transfer the pork shank and rinse it in cold tap water. We take this step whenever we make Chinese

soups with pork shank or any other bones and meat.
2. Soak 1 piece of chenpi in cold water for 20 minutes. Wash the dried jujubes with cold running tap water. Make the rest of the ingredients as listed.
3. Pressure cooker soup; place all the ingredients into the pressure cooker. Pour 2 liters of cold running tap water into the pot. Do not add any salt. Keep pressure cooks at high pressure for 30 minutes.
4. Heat up the pressure cooker to bring the soup back to a full boil. Add sea salt to taste. Serve hot.

Nutritional Information

- Preparation Time: 60 minutes
- Total Servings: 6-8
- Calories: 115
- Total Fat: 12.1g
- Carbohydrates: 13.7g
- Protein: 5g

Italian Chicken Sausage Soup

Ingredients

- 2 tsp olive oil
- 4 turkey sausage
- 1 diced onion
- 3 minced garlic cloves
- ½ cup pearl barley
- 1 cup green lentils
- 1 piece chicken breast
- ½ cup fresh parsley
- 3 cups chicken stock
- 15 ounces (420 g) garbanzo beans
- 1 cup mild salsa
- 16 ounces (450 g) fresh spinach

Preparation Method

1. Heat 1 teaspoon olive oil in the instant pot over medium heat. Add sausage meat, and cook until browned, breaking it into crumbles

2. Transfer sausage to a plate and drain oil. Add another one teaspoon of olive oil to pressure cooker, cook onion, and garlic until onion is transparent
3. Add barley and mix 1 minute. Return sausage to instant pot. Add chicken, lentils, parsley, and chicken stock to cooker, adding enough stock to cover chicken completely
4. Close cover securely places pressure regulator on vent pipe. Bring pressure cooker to full pressure over high heat (this may take 15 minutes)
5. Reduce heat to medium-high, cook for 9 minutes. Pressure regulator should maintain a slow, steady rocking motion; adjust temperature if necessary.
6. Remove instant pot from heat, use quick-release following manufacturer's instructions or allow pressure to drop on its own
7. Open instant pot and transfer chicken, shred meat and return to soup. Add garbanzo beans, spinach, and salsa. Stir to blend and heat through before serving

Nutritional Information

- Preparation Time: 50 minutes
- Total Servings: 8
- Calories: 245
- Fat: 3.3
- Carbohydrates: 37.3
- Protein: 17.4

Minestrone Soup

Ingredients

- 1 cup cooked white beans
- 1 pound (450g) cooked ground beef
- 1 diced potato
- 2 diced carrots
- 2 diced celery stalks
- 1 chopped onion
- 2 garlic cloves
- 2 pounds (1kg) chicken Broth
- 2 pounds (1kg) crushed tomatoes
- 2 tsp tomato paste
- 1 tsp salt
- Italian seasoning (as needed for taste)

Preparation Method

1. Mix all ingredients in the instant pot.
2. Put pressure cooker on manual high pressure for 20 minutes.
3. Let depressurize for 10 minutes.

Nutritional Information

- Preparation Time: 30 minutes
- Total Servings: 4-6
- Calories: 367
- Fat: 14.2g
- Carbohydrates: 45.6g
- Protein: 18.2g

Chicken Lentil Soup

Ingredients

- 1 lb (450g) dried lentils
- 12 oz (340g) chicken thighs
- 7 cups water
- 1 small onion
- 2 chopped scallions
- 1/4 cup chopped cilantro
- 3 cloves garlic
- 1 medium ripe tomato
- 1 tsp garlic powder
- 1 tsp cumin
- ½ tsp oregano
- 1 tsp paprika
- 1 tsp salt

Preparation Method

1. Place all the ingredients in the cooker, stir and cover.
2. Press "Soup" button and cook 30 minutes.
3. When ready and the pressure releases, shred the chicken and stir. It makes about 11 cups.

Nutritional Information

- Preparation Time: 45 minutes
- Total Servings: 11 cups
- Calories: 129
- Fat: 2.5g
- Carbohydrates: 16g
- Protein: 1.5g

Kale Soup

Ingredients

- 1 small chopped onion
- 3.5 ounces (100g) kale
- 1 ounce (28g) coconut or almond milk
- 1 tsp ground garlic
- 3.5 ounces (100g) ground sausage
- 1.8 ounces (50g) potatoes
- 1 tbsp thyme
- 8 tbsp chicken stock
- Red pepper and salt (as needed)
- Topping: Parmesan cheese

Preparation Method

1. Put onion, garlic and ground sausage and press Sauté button.
2. Add potatoes and seasoning (thyme, salt, a little crushed red pepper) and chicken stock, stir well.

3. Hit soup button and set timer for 25 minutes, add chopped kale and a free coconut/almond milk, continue to heat on "Sauté" if needed.
4. Serve topped with a little Parmesan. It tastes great next day also.

Nutritional Information

- Preparation Time: 30 minutes
- Total Servings: 3
- Calories: 266
- Total Fat: 17g
- Carbohydrates: 16.1g
- Protein: 10.6g

Beef Quinoa Soup

Ingredients

- 2 tbsp olive oil
- 6 chopped scallions
- 2 cloves garlic
- 1 tomato
- 1/2 tsp cumin
- 1/3 tsp homemade seasonings
- 8 ounces (225g) beef (cubed into small pieces)
- 5 cups water
- 1 carrot
- 1 tbsp yellow bell pepper
- 2 medium potatoes
- 1 cup cooked quinoa
- 2 tbsp fresh cilantro
- Salt and pepper (to taste)

Preparation Method

1. Sauté oil in a pressure cooker; add scallions and garlic and Sauté until soft over medium heat, about 3 minutes. Add tomato, cumin,

season with achiote, 1/4 cup cilantro and cook another 2 minutes.
2. Add water, beef, bullion, carrot, bell pepper, salt and bring to a boil. Cook on low about 45 minutes, until meat is tender.
3. Add cooked quinoa and potato, and cook an additional 10 minutes. Add remaining chopped cilantro and serve.

Nutritional Information

- Preparation Time: 60 minutes
- Total Servings: 4
- Calories: 307.9
- Fat: 13.8g
- Carbohydrates: 31.3g
- Protein: 15.7g

Turkey Mixed Bean Soup

Ingredients

- 1 tbsp extra virgin light olive oil
- 1 large onion
- 1 carrot
- 1 celery stalk
- 1/2 cup chopped parsley
- 3 cloves garlic
- 6 cups water
- 1 smoked turkey drumstick
- 2 bay leaves
- 2 cups dried black beans
- 1/2 tsp fresh ground black pepper
- 1 tsp coarse salt

Preparation Method

1. Place the onions, carrots, celery and parsley and olive oil in an electric pressure cooker over medium-high heat and cook until fragrant, about 8 to 10 minutes.
2. Add the garlic and cook 1 minute.
3. Add turkey leg, water, bay leaves, beans, and black pepper and bring to boil. Cook for 45 minutes. Drop bay leaves and set turkey legs aside.
4. Discard skin from the turkey leg and cut the meat off the bone into bite-size pieces.
5. Using a blender, puree the beans leaving the soup chunky, or to your desired consistency.
6. If you use a traditional blender, blend in batches and return the beans to the pot after beans are pureed. Or use an immersion blender.
7. Add the salt and place the turkey in the soup.

Nutritional Information

- Preparation Time: 55 minutes
- Total Servings: 8
- Calories: 133
- Fat: 2g
- Carbohydrates: 26g

Pepe Beef Soup

Ingredients

- 1 pound (450g) lean ground beef
- 1/3 tsp salt
- 1/2 cup diced onion
- 1/2 cup diced celery
- 1/2 cup diced carrot
- 2 pounds (900g) tomatoes
- 2 pounds (900g) beef stock
- 2 bay leaves
- 4 ounces (115g) small pasta
- Optional: grated Parmesan cheese

Preparation Method

1. Use the Sauté button, add salt and the ground beef. Cook until browned breaking the meat up into small pieces as it cooks. When cooked, add the onion, celery, and carrots and Sauté 3 to 4 minutes.

2. Add the beef stock, tomatoes, and bay leaves. Close and using a pressure cooker and select soup (35 minutes).
3. Make the quick release, once the pressure is out to open, add the pasta and stir, cover and press manual pressure 6 minutes. Remove bay leaves and serve.

Nutritional Information

- Preparation Time: 45 minutes
- Total Servings: 6
- Calories: 249
- Fat: 8g
- Carbohydrates: 23g
- Protein: 24

Bacon Spinach Soup

Ingredients

- 3 pounds (1.4kg)navy beans
- 4 slices bacon
- 1 onion
- 1 carrot
- 1 celery stalk
- 2 tbsp tomato paste
- 4 cups chicken broth
- 2 bay leaves
- 1 spring fresh rosemary
- 3 cups baby spinach

Preparation Method

1. In a blender, blend the beans with 1 cup of water.
2. Press Sauté button, then cooks the bacon until crisp. Set aside on paper towels.

3. Add the celery, onion, and carrots to the pot and cook until soft, about 5 minutes. Stir in the tomato paste, then adds the bay leaves, pureed beans, broth, rosemary.
4. Cook on high pressure 15 minutes. Let the pressure release, remove bay leaves and rosemary.
5. Put 2 cups of the soup in the blender and puree to thicken, then add to the soup the spinach and stir until wilted.
6. Serve with bacon.

Nutritional Information

- Preparation Time: 20 minutes
- Total Servings: 6 cups
- Calories: 211
- Fat: 1.5g
- Carbohydrates: 39g
- Protein: 15g

Mango Dal

Ingredients

- 1 tbsp coconut oil
- ½ tsp ground cumin
- 1 medium onion
- 4 cloves garlic
- 1 tbsp minced fresh ginger
- ½ tsp ground coriander
- ¼ tsp cayenne pepper
- ½ tsp sea salt
- 1 cup Chana Dal
- 4 cups chicken broth
- 5 ground turmeric
- 2 peeled and diced mangos
- 1/2 cup chopped fresh cilantro
- 1/2 lime juice

Preparation Method

1. Put dal in a colander and rinse until water is clear.
2. Set the instant pot to Sauté. Heat coconut oil, add cumin and Sauté until fragrant, about 30 seconds.
3. Add onion, Sauté until soft and starting to brown. Add ginger, garlic, coriander, cayenne, and sea salt and Sauté for 1 minute more.
4. Add the dal, chicken broth, and turmeric in the pot. Keep on the Sauté feature and bring to a boil and boil for about 10 minutes.
5. Add mangoes. Place the lid on the pressure cooker. Press the Beans/Chili button, adjust the time to 20 minutes. After naturally released, stir in lime juice and cilantro.
6. Serve over cooked rice.

Nutritional Information

- Preparation Time: 30 minutes
- Total Servings: 4-6
- Calories: 17
- Fat: 2.5g
- Carbohydrates: 26.4g
- Protein: 8.4

Chicken Tortilla Soup

Ingredients

- 1 1/4 pounds (570g). raw boneless skinless chicken breasts
- 4 tomatoes
- 5 green chili peppers
- 1 cup corn
- 1 cup black beans
- 1 medium onion
- 1 jalapeno
- 2 cloves garlic
- 4 cups of chicken stock
- 1 tsp ground cumin
- 1 tsp chili powder
- 1 tsp salt

- 1/4 tsp black pepper
  Corn tortillas
- 3 tbsp vegetable oil

Preparation Method

1. In a small pan, combine chili powder, cumin, pepper, and salt. Liberally rub over chicken breasts before putting in Instant Pot.
2. Dice the jalapeno, peppers, and tomato, put on top of chicken.
3. Pour chicken broth over the whole mixture.
4. Cook for 15 minutes. Then do a quick pressure release. Shred the chicken with two forks.
5. Make the tortilla strips by preheating your oven to 350 and cut the corn tortillas into strips.
6. Graze with vegetable oil and sprinkle with salt.
7. Bake for about 10-15 minutes.
8. Stir soup together and serve with tortilla strips as garnish

Pea Lentil Soup

Ingredients

- 1 cup red lentil
- 1 cup yellow split peas
- 1 chopped onion
- 2 chopped carrots
- 5 chopped garlic cloves
- 1 tsp ground cumin
- 8 cups chicken broth
- Salt and pepper (as needed)
- 1 tsp lemon juice

Preparation Method

1. Place the split peas, lentils, carrots, onion, garlic, and cumin into a pressure cooker, and stir in the chicken broth.
2. Cook under pressure for 30 minutes. Remove from heat, and allow pressure to cool.
3. When the cooker is at normal, open and season with salt and pepper and stirs in lemon juice to serve.

Nutritional Information

- Preparation Time: 40 minutes
- Total Servings: 10
- Calories: 170
- Fat: 0.7g
- Carbohydrates: 29.4g
- Protein: 11.6g

Broccoli Cheddar Soup

Ingredients

- 2 tbsp butter
- 1 small yellow onion
- 4 chicken stock
- 1 large bunch broccoli
- 1/4 tsp garlic powder
- 1 shredded carrots
- 1 heavy cream
- 2 shredded sharp cheddar cheese

Preparation Method

1. Dice onion and carrot.
2. Break broccoli up into small florets. Turn your Instant Pot to sauté. Add butter and heat until sizzling.
3. Sauté diced onion until translucent.
4. Add carrots, broccoli florets, chicken stock, garlic powder, and onion powder, to pot
5. Cook on the manual setting high pressure for 5 minutes.

6. Then do a quick pressure release.
7. Stir in the sharp cheddar cheese and the heavy cream.
8. Serve.

Tomato Soup

Ingredients

- 1/3 cup extra-virgin olive oil
- 4 carrots
- 1 yellow onion
- 1 tbsp dried basil
- 3.28 ounces (90g) canned tomatoes
- 1 cup chicken broth
- 1/2 cup heavy whipping cream

Preparation Method

1. Dice the onion finely and chop the carrot into half-inch bits.
2. Select Sauté on Instant Pot and allow it to heat.
3. Add the oil, carrots, onions and dried basil. And the onions become a bit translucent. Sauté until vegetables start to caramelize
4. Add canned tomatoes and chicken broth. Cook at High Pressure for 5 minutes.

5. When Beep is sound, allow a full Natural Pressure Release.
6. Turn to Sauté.
7. Use a blender and blend until soup is smooth.
8. Add cream and allow to heat through.
9. Serve

Chicken Noodle Soup

Ingredients

- 1 tbsp butter
- 1/2 medium yellow onion
- 4 cloves of garlic
- 5 carrots
- 2 celery stalks
- 1 whole 5 pounds (2kg) chicken
- 2 tbsp of soy sauce
- 8 cups of water
- 3 tbsp cornstarch
- 4 ounces (115g) of extra wide egg noodles

Preparation Method

1. Turn Instant Pot to the Sauté function.
2. Dice onions, carrots, celery, and mince garlic.
3. Heat butter and drop in the onions, sautéing them until they just start to soften.

4. Drop in the garlic, carrots, and celery and sauté, stirring for about a minute until they are coated in the flour.
5. Carefully insert the whole chicken to Instant Pot (breast side up)
6. Pour the water and soy sauce over top of it.
7. Cook on the manual setting, High Pressure for 20 or so minutes.
8. When it beeps do a Quick pressure release.
9. Carefully remove the chicken and put on a cutting board.
10. Turn Pot back to the Sauté function bring to a boil.
11. Remove a portion of the broth and put in a bowl.
12. Whisk the cornstarch into the reserved broth until smooth.
13. Slowly pour cornstarch mixture into the boiling broth.
14. Carefully stir the egg noodles in and cook until just done.
15. Break the chicken up, shredding the dark meat and chopping up the breasts
16. Discard the bones and skin.
17. Place the chicken in the soup and sprinkle with the fresh parsley.
18. Serve.

Baked Potato Soup

Ingredients

- 3 tbsp minced onion or 1 large minced shallot
- 5-pound (2kg) bag potatoes, peeled and cubed
- 6 cups chicken broth
- 2 cups milk
- 2 cups shredded cheddar cheese
- 1/3 cup sour cream
- 1/3 cup softened cream cheese
- 1 bag real bacon bits
- 4 tbsp butter
- 1 green onion, cubed; for garnish
- Salt and pepper; to taste

Preparation Method

1. Place the potatoes and minced shallots in the instant pot and then cover it with enough chicken broth.
2. Securely cover the lid and cook on soup or manual setting for about 10 minutes.
3. Once ready, rotate the valve to venting so that pressure can naturally be released.
4. Open the lid and then use an electric hand mixer or a potato masher to crush the potatoes.
5. Now, add cheddar cheese, butter, cream cheese, sour cream, salt, and pepper and then blend until it reaches the consistency you prefer.
6. Pour the milk into the soup, and if desirable, you can add salt and pepper.
7. Serve and top with the toppings

Cook Time: 10 minutes

Servings: 8

Minestrone Soup

Ingredients

- 2 tbsp. lard or olive oil
- 2 stalks celery, diced
- 1 large onion, diced
- 1 large carrot, diced
- 3 cloves garlic, minced
- 1 tsp. dried oregano
- 1 tsp. dried basil
- Sea salt and pepper, to taste
- 28 ounces. (800g) can San Marzano tomatoes
- 15 ounces (425g) can (or about 2 cups freshly cooked, drained) white or cannellini beans
- 1 bay leaf
- 1 cup gluten-free elbow pasta
- 4 cups bone broth or vegetable broth
- 1/2 cup fresh kale or spinach (without the rib) torn into shreds
- 1/3 cup finely grated Parmesan cheese

- 1-2 tbsp fresh pesto (optional)

Preparation Method

1. Set Instant Pot to saute mode.
2. Add olive oil, onion, carrot, celery and
3. Add basil, oregano, salt, and pepper.
4. If canned tomatoes are still whole, mix tomatoes and liquid in the can in a food processor or blender to dice tomatoes.
5. Add other ingredients (pasta, bone broth, bay leaf, tomatoes, and spinach or kale). Lock the lid and set to manual high pressure for 6 minutes. It will take about 8 minutes for the instant pot to reach high pressure; then it will cook for 6 minutes.
6. When the timer beeps, let sit for about one minute. Then set to quick pressure release to vent steam.
7. Add white kidney beans.
8. Serve in bowls and garnish with pesto and Parmesan cheese.

Turkey Noodle Soup

Ingredients

- 1 tbsp butter
- 1 large onion, diced
- 4 carrot, peeled and cut into ¼-inch thick rounds
- 1 celery rib, diced
- 6 cup turkey stock
- 2 cups diced turkey
- 1 tbsp salt
- Fresh ground pepper
- Egg noodles, cooked according to package directions

Preparation Method

1. Set Saute and add butter to the Instant Pot. Then Butter is melted, add the onion and cook, occasionally stirring until the onion starts to soften about 1 minute.
2. Add the celery and carrots, and saute for about 5 minutes stirring occasionally.
3. Add turkey stock and turkey. Lock lid in place. Select Hight Pressure. Set timer for 5 minutes. When the timer goes off, wait 5 minutes and then use a quick pressure release to release pressure. When valve drops, carefully remove the lid. Add salt and pepper to taste.
4. Serve soup spooned over prepared egg noodles.

Cauliflower Potato Soup

Ingredients

- 1 pound (450g) potatoes cored and peeled
- 1 medium head of cauliflower
- 1/2 pound (225g) bacon, chopped
- 4 cloves garlic, chopped fine
- 4 cups chicken broth
- 1 cup whole milk
- 1 tbsp salt
- 1/2 tbsp pepper
- 1 ½ cut grated cheddar cheese

Preparation Method

1. Set Instant Pot to Saute. Press the "+ajust" button
2. Prep and add in bacon and garlic. Cook about 5 minutes (until bacon is cooked to slightly browned).

3. Add the chicken stock peeled potatoes, and chopped cauliflower. Set the lid on and push vent to seal.
4. Press MANUAL button and cook for 10 minutes on high pressure. Turn pot off.
5. Natural release for 10 minutes. Then quick release until the pressure is released.
6. Remove the instant pot lid. Add in the milk and 1 ¼ cup of the cheese. Mash the potatoes and cauliflower with the potato masher or immersion blender. You can add more broth.
7. Serve with bacon crumbles and remaining cheese shreds on top as desired.

Easy Cream of Broccoli Soup

Ingredients

- 4 cups of steamed broccoli florets and steams (fresh or frozen)
- 5 cups chicken broth
- 6 tbsp butter
- 1/3 cup all-purpose organic unbleached and unenriched flour
- 2/3cup organic half & half
- Salt and pepper to taste

Preparation Method

1. Started with steamed broccoli –steam for 2-3 minutes.
2. In the Instant Pot combine butter with the ¼ c flour and work into a thick paste on the Saute function. Be careful and not to let the butter burn.
3. Add the chicken broth and frequently stir on the Saute function until it thickens from the roux.

4. In the meantime, drain the broccoli and cut into small peace.
5. Add the broccoli and stir until combined.
6. Add the half & half and let thicken as you turn the pot off.
7. Add salt and pepper to taste.

Chapter 5. Vegetarian Soup Recipes

Butternut Squash Curry Soup

Ingredients

- A bit of olive oil for sauteing (optional)
- 2 cloves of garlic - peeled and roughly chopped
- 1 large onion, diced
- 1 - 1.5 pounds butternut squash, roughly chopped
- 1 tsp ginger
- 1 tsp cumin
- 1 tsp garam masala
- 1/2 tsp cayenne (more or less to taste)
- 1 quart vegetable broth

- 1 cup lentils, rinsed and picked over
- 1 can diced tomatoes, not drained (1.5-2 cups of tomatoes)
- Cilantro (optional) - for topping

Preparation Method

1. Click the "Saute" button and add olive oil. Saute the garlic and onion for about 3-5 minutes or until starting to brown.
2. Add the butternut squash and spices (cumin, ginger, cayenne and garam masala) and mix well - allowing the butternut squash to soften lightly for about 2 - 3 minutes.
3. Add the vegetable broth and lentils.
4. Lock the lid and put the pressure valve to "sealed."
5. Press the Manual button and adjust to 6 minutes on high pressure
6. Instant pot will come to pressure and cook for 6 minutes
7. After it beeps, let it be in Keep Warm for about 10 minutes. Release any remaining pressure with the pressure valve.
8. Stir in the tomatoes.
9. Blend until completely creamy.
10. Serve topped with cilantro (optional).

Pure Black Beans Soup

Ingredients

- 7 cups water
- 1 pound (450g) black beans
- 1 chopped onion
- 1 tbsp chopped cilantro
- 1 tbsp olive oil
- Salt and pepper to taste
- 2 tbsp vinegar

Preparation Method

1. Combine black beans, water, onion, cilantro, olive oil, and salt in a pressure cooker
2. Cook on high pressure about 40 minutes
3. Open the lid and stir balsamic vinegar into beans

Nutritional Information

- Preparation Time: 50 minutes
- Total Servings: 8

- Calories: 216
- Fat: 2.5g
- Carbohydrates: 37g
- Protein: 12.5g

Mushroom Milk Soup

Ingredients

- 2 tbsp vegetable oil
- 8 ounces (225g) mushrooms
- 1/4 cup vegetable broth
- 2 and 3/4 cup water
- 2 ounces (56g) almond flour
- 4 tbsp vegetable butter
- 1/4 cup soy milk

Preparation Method

1. Add oil to pressure cooker and press Sauté button. Add sliced mushroom to cooker. Add chicken or beef broth. Continue to cook down until mushroom appears darker in color.
2. Add water and close lid. Slide lever to the "Pressurize" mode. As soon as the cooker is pressurized, switch to quick release. Drain broth and mushroom in a colander and save broth. Place mushrooms back.

3. Add butter to a saucepan and melt to a slight simmer. Add all-purpose flour slowly and constantly whisking until it smells like pie crust.
4. Slowly add mushroom broth until all clumps are dissolved, and there is a creamy texture. Add milk and boil. Then add mushrooms and bring to a simmer. Continue to whisk occasionally and simmer for about 8 min.
5. Remove from pan and enjoy the taste. Serve over noodles, rice or as soup. It tastes like cream of mushroom soup.

Nutritional Information

- Preparation Time: 25 minutes
- Total Servings: 4
- Calories: 278
- Fat: 6.8g
- Carbohydrates: 24.111
- Protein: 1.4g

Baby Potato Soup

Ingredients

- 2 pounds (900g) potatoes
- 3/4 cup baby carrots
- 12 cloves roasted garlic
- 1/2 cup celery
- 1/2 cup fresh baby spinach leaves
- 1 cup onion
- 1 cup vegetable broth
- 1 tbsp fresh basil leaves
- 1/4 tsp crushed red pepper
- 1/4 tsp paprika
- 1 tbsp ground flax or chia seeds
- 1/4 tsp Salt
- Garnish: cheddar cheese, fresh basil leaves

Preparation Method

1. Place all ingredients in the pressure cooker and stir. Press the soup button and leave the time set for 30 minutes.

2. When the cooker beeps, throw a kitchen towel over the lid and do a quick pressure release. Use an immersion blender, and apply short zaps until the soup is thick but still has some chunky carrot and potato pieces.
3. Ladle into bowls and garnish with basil and cheese.
4. Serve with freshly baked whole grain wheat bread or cornbread.

Nutritional Information

- Preparation Time: 35 minutes
- Total Servings: 8 cups
- Calories: 150
- Fat: 3.2g
- Carbohydrates: 34.3g
- Protein: 8.4g

Sweet Potatoes, Kale and Yellow Split-Pea Soup

Ingredients

- 8 cups water
- 1 tbsp black mustard seeds
- 2 medium onions, chopped
- 1 1/2 tbsp whole cumin
- 2 tbsp finely minced garlic
- 2 medium sweet potatoes, peeled and cubed
- 3 cups yellow split peas, dried, picked over and rinsed
- 1-2 tbsp mild curry powder; to taste
- 1 tbsp finely minced fresh ginger or ginger paste
- Salt to taste (optional)
- 1 bunch kale

Preparation Method

1. Sauté onions in a large pressure cooker for about 5 minutes and add a tablespoon of water

to avoid sticking. Add a pinch of baking soda so that the onions can cook quicker. Once they are almost translucent, add mustard seeds, and cumin then stirs well and cook for about 60 seconds.
2. Pour garlic and ginger into the mixture and cook for an additional 60 seconds then add split peas, sweet potatoes, curry powder (1 tablespoon) and water, stir well to combine.
3. Securely close the lid and cook at high pressure for about ten minutes.
4. When ready, remove from heat and let the pressure naturally release for about 15 minutes before doing a quick release.
5. Meanwhile, wash kale then remove and throw away the hard central rib. Slice the leaves roughly.
6. When split peas cooked, place kale into the pot and season with salt and curry powder to taste.
7. If the kale is tender, continue cooking it on low heat for about 10 minutes. If it retains some crunch, don't heat the pot but leave it covered for between 5-10 minutes.

Nutrition Information per Serving:

- Cook Time: 30 minutes
- Servings: 8
- Calories 309,
- Carbohydrates 57g,
- Fat 2g,
- Protein 20g,
- Fiber 21g a
- Sodium 28mg

Spicy Vegetable Soup

Ingredients

- 1 cup celery
- 1/2 cup carrots
- 1 medium onion
- 1 fresh jalapeno
- 2 tbsp olive oil
- 1/2 tsp coriander seeds
- 1/4 tsp cumin seed
- 3 big russet potatoes
- 2 tbsp vegetable broth
- 4 cups water
- 1/4 tsp ground turmeric
- 1/4 tsp ground cumin
- 2 tbsp chopped jalapenos
- Optional: chopped cilantro

Preparation Method

1. Set pressure cooker on Sauté. Add olive oil and heat for a minute.
2. Drop in cumin seeds and coriander seeds, and heat until the coriander seeds pop. Add the chopped celery, carrots onion, and jalapeno.
3. Sauté until the onions become translucent, about 5 minutes. Add the pickled jalapenos, turmeric, cumin. When you fill some nice aroma, put in the chicken broth and potatoes.
4. Change the setting to soup and set for 30 minutes. Let pressure come to normal. Before serving add in the chopped cilantro. Serve with good bread.

Nutritional Information

- Preparation Time: 35 minutes
- Total Servings: 4
- Calories: 155
- Total Fat: 11.2g
- Carbohydrates: 9.9g
- Protein: 5.4g

Veggie-Quinoa Soup

Ingredients

- 3 cups boiling water
- 2 bags of frozen mixed vegetables (12 ounces each)
- 1 can of white beans (15 ounces)
- 1 can of fire-roasted diced tomatoes (15 ounces)
- 1 can of pinto beans (15 ounces)
- ¼ cups rinsed quinoa
- 1 tbsp dried basil
- 1 tbsp minced garlic
- 1 tbsp hot sauce
- ½ tbsp dried oregano
- Dash of black pepper
- Dash of salt

Preparation Method

1. Combine all the ingredients in the pot.
2. Close and seal the lid.
3. Select "Manual, and set time to 2 minutes on high pressure.

4. When time is up, hit "cancel" and quick-release the pressure.
5. When all the pressure is gone, open the cooker and season to taste.
6. Serve

Nutritional Information

- Total calories: 201
- Protein: 11
- Carbs: 37
- Fiber: 11
- Fat: 1.1

Chipotle Pumpkin Soup

Serving 6

Ingredients

- 1 onion, diced roughly
- 3 cloves of garlic, diced roughly
- 1 tsp cinnamon
- 1/4 tsp nutmeg
- 1 tsp salt
- 1 tsp black pepper
- 1 chipotle pepper in adobe sauce - seed the pepper
- 1 tbsp adobe sauce from the chipotle pepper
- 2 cups red potatoes, diced
- 2 cups of green apple, diced
- 1 15-ounces can of pumpkin puree (or 1.5 cups of cooked fresh pumpkin)
- 1/4 cup uncooked red lentils, pulsed or chopped into small pieces
- 1/4 cup walnuts (or almonds), pulsed or chopped into small pieces
- 2 cups vegetable broth
- 2 cups water

Preparation Method

1. Saute the onion and garlic about 3 - 4 minutes, until starting to brown.
2. Add the spices (cinnamon, nutmeg, salt, black pepper, chipotle chili and adobe sauce) and stir well.
3. Add the potatoes, apples, pumpkin puree, ground red lentils, ground walnuts, vegetable broth, and water.
4. Click the Manual button and reduce the cooking time to 4 minutes over high pressure.
5. Once cooking is complete, let naturally release for 10 minutes and then release any remaining pressure.
6. Carefully open the lid and transfer the soup to a blender or food processor. (You can use an immersion blender).
7. Blend until completely smooth.
8. Serve warm.

Mexican Baked Potato Soup

Ingredients

- 4 – 5 cloves garlic, diced
- 1 large onion, diced
- 1/8 -1/2 cup jalapeno seeded, diced (to taste)
- 4 cups vegetable broth
- 4 cups potatoes, diced
- ½ cup of salsa of choice (
- 1 tsp cumin
- ¼ tsp oregano
- ¼ tsp garlic powder
- green onions, to taste
- ½ cup nutritional yeast (or to taste)
- Tofutti better than sour cream, to taste (optional)
- black pepper and white pepper, to taste

Preparation Method

1. Press the Saute button. Add onion, garlic, and jalapenos and saute until brown.
2. Turn off the Saute. Add the vegetable broth, potatoes, salsa, cumin, oregano and garlic powder – stir well.
3. Lock the lid and put it on "Sealed". Click the Manual button and set the timer for 10 minutes.
4. When the beeper sounds, allow the pressure to come down naturally. After about 20 minutes you can release any remaining pressure and open the lid carefully – away from you.
5. If you want the chunky soup, stop now and stir in the green onions, nutritional yeast, and pepper. Top each serving with Tofutti if desired.
6. If you want the creamy soup
7. Carefully transfer the soup to a blender. Add the nutritional yeast and pepper to the blender. Blend until smooth. Stir in the green onions. Top each serving with Tofutti if desired.
8. Serve warm or cold

Lentil Red Curry & Coconut Milk Soup

Ingredients

- 3 cloves of garlic, minced
- 1 large onion, diced
- 2 tbsp red curry paste
- 1/8 tsp ginger powder
- pinch of red pepper flakes (optional)
- 1 15-ounces can of coconut milk
- 1 14-ounces can of diced tomatoes (do not drain)
- 2 cups of vegetable broth
- 1 1/2 cups of lentils
- chopped spinach to taste (optional)

Preparation Method

1. Press the Saute button and wait until warm.
2. Add the garlic and onion. Saute until beginning to brown. If it starts to stick, add a bit of vegetable broth.

3. Turn off the Saute.
4. Add the red pepper flakes, red curry paste, and ginger powder, and stir well.
5. Add the coconut milk, diced tomatoes, vegetable broth and lentils. Stir well again.
6. Close the lid. Click the Manual button and reduce the time to 6 minutes.
7. Let the pressure release naturally. After it has released, open the lid and stir in the chopped spinach.
8. Serve and enjoy!

Taco Soup

Ingredients

- 3 - 4 cloves of garlic, minced
- 1 large onion, diced
- 2 cans (15-ounces) of black beans, drained and rinsed
- 2 cans (15-ounces) of diced tomatoes, not drained
- 2 cans (15-ounces) of tomato sauce
- 2 cans (12-ounces) filled with water
- 1 cup frozen corn (or 1 can)
- 1 cup frozen chopped spinach (or fresh)
- 1/4 cup cilantro, diced (optional)
- 1 tbsp paprika
- 3 tbsp chili powder
- 1/2 tbsp cumin
- a dash of chipotle chili powder (optional)
- 1 tbsp chipotle hot sauce (optional)

Preparation Method

1. Press the Saute button. Once it's warm, add the garlic and onion, saute until brown. Add a bit of water if it starts to stick.
2. Turn off the Saute.
3. Add the remaining ingredients and stir well.
4. Close the lid. Turn the valve to "sealed". Click the Manual button and reduce the time to 3 minutes.
5. Once the cycle is complete, allow the pressure come down for at least 10 minutes before releasing. Stir well.
6. Serve warm.

Sweet Potato and Red Curry Soup

Ingredients

- 1 large onion, diced
- 2 cloves of garlic, minced
- 2 tbsp chili powder
- 1.5 pounds of sweet potatoes, diced
- 1 cup of dried brown lentils
- 1 tsp sea salt
- 4 cups of vegetable broth
- 2 cans (15-ounces) of kidney beans (cooked!), drained and rinsed
- 2 tbsp red curry paste
- 1 can (15-ounces) of coconut milk
- 28 ounces of diced tomatoes, not drained
- 1/2 cup of cilantro, cut into small pieces
- 1 tbsp lime juice
- 1 can green chilis

Preparation Method

1. Press the Saute button to heat the instant pot.
2. Add olive oil. Add the garlic and onion and saute about 5 minutes until they begin to soften.
3. Add the sweet potatoes to the garlic and onions.
4. Click "Cancel" to stop the sautéing feature
5. Add rest ingredients to the instant pot
6. Close the lid. Put the steam valve to "sealed".
7. Click "Manual" and reduce the time to 10 minutes
8. Once the cooking cycle is complete, let the pressure release naturally from the instant pot
9. After the pressure has released, open the lid and stir well
10. Serve warm

Sweet Potato and Peanut Butter Soup

Ingredients

- a bit of oil for sautéing
- 3 cloves of garlic, chopped
- 1 large onion, roughly chopped
- 1 15-ounces can diced tomatoes, not drained
- 3 large sweet potatoes, cut into 1 - 2 inch cubes
- 1 4-ounces can green chilis
- 1 14-ounces can of full-fat coconut milk
- 1/4 tsp ground ginger
- 1/2 tsp allspice
- 1 tbsp lime juice
- 2 cups vegetable broth
- 1/2 cup peanut butter
- cilantro to taste
- black pepper to taste

Preparation Method

1. Press the Saute button to heat the instant pot. Add oil, if desired.
2. Add onion and garlic. Saute until softened, stirring constantly.
3. Turn off the Saute.
4. Add all of the resting ingredients. Stir well.
5. Close the lid. Turn the valve to "Sealed".
6. Use Manual and set the timer for 4 minutes.
7. Once the cooking cycle is complete, let the pressure release naturally from the instant pot. After the pressure has released, open the lid and stir well.
8. Blend the soup to your desired consistency, using caution, as it will be hot.
9. Serve warm, with crusty (gluten-free) bread, and a nice light salad

Cabbage Leek Diet Soup

Ingredients

- 1/2 head cabbage, chopped
- 2-3 leeks, carefully cleaned and chopped
- 2 tbsp coconut oil
- 3-4 ribs of celery, diced
- 1 bell pepper, diced
- 2-3 carrots, diced
- 2/3 cloves of garlic, minced
- 4 cups vegetable broth
- 1 tsp Italian seasoning
- 1 tsp Creole seasoning
- black pepper to taste
- 2-3 cups of mixed salad greens

Preparation Method

1. Heat coconut oil on sauté setting in Instant Pot.
2. Add prepared vegetables (except salad greens) one at a time, starting with carrots, stirring well after each addition.

3. Save garlic for last, so it doesn't burn.
4. Season with black pepper, Creole seasoning, and Italian seasoning.
5. Add vegetable broth.
6. Close vent and cook on soup setting for 20 minutes.
7. Once the cooking is complete, open vent and remove the lid.
8. Add salad greens, stir well and let sit a few minutes to wilt.
9. Taste and adjust seasonings if needed.

Curried Butternut Squash Soup

Time: 20 minutes / Servings: 6

Ingredients

For Soup

- 1 butternut squash peeled and cubed
- 1 large onion chopped
- 2 cloves garlic chopped
- 1 tsp fresh ginger minced
- 2 tsp curry powder
- 2 tsp olive oil
- 1 can (14.5-ounces) coconut milk
- 4 cups vegetable stock
- Salt and pepper to taste

For roasted seeds

- 1 cup squash seeds washed
- 2 tsp olive oil

- 1 tsp cumin
- 1/2 tsp cinnamon
- Salt and pepper to taste

Preparation Method

For Soup

1. Press the Saute button on the instant pot and add the olive oil
2. Saute the onions until softened. Add the ginger, garlic, curry powder, salt, and pepper. Stir for 1-2 minutes.
3. Add the butternut squash cubes and saute for 2 minutes.
4. Add the vegetable stock and coconut milk.
5. Lock the lid and cook on high pressure for 12 minutes.
6. When the instant pot beeps, let it cool for 5 minutes before releasing the pressure.
7. Blend the soup until creamy.
8. Add more salt and pepper if needed.

For Seeds

1. Preheat oven to 350F
2. In a bowl, mix all the ingredients.
3. Line a sheet pan with aluminum foil
4. Spread the seeds on the sheet pan.
5. Bake for about 20 minutes until crispy.
6. Top the soup with seeds and enjoy!

Spicy Collards and Black-eyed Pea Soup

Time 1 hour 5 minutes / Servings 6

Ingredients

- 6 cups water
- 2 ribs celery, diced
- 2 onions, diced
- 3-4 cloves garlic, minced
- 1 cup diced green bell pepper
- 1 pound collard greens, tough stems removed and greens chopped
- 2 cups dried black-eyed peas, picked over and rinsed
- 1.5 tsp dried thyme (divided)
- 1 tsp oregano (divided)
- 1 16-ounces can tomatoes (fire-roasted preferred)
- 1 tablespoon hot sauce
- 1/4 tsp cayenne (to taste)
- 1/2 tsp chipotle pepper (to taste)
- 1/2 tsp smoked Spanish paprika

- 1-2 tsp salt (to taste)
- 1 tbsp double strength tomato paste (or 2 tbsp. regulars)
- 1/4 tsp black pepper
- additional water (or vegetable broth), as needed

Preparation Method

1. Press Sauté button on your Instant Pot. Add the onion. Sauté for about 5 minutes. Add the garlic, celery, and green pepper, and cook, stirring, for 3 more minutes.
2. Add the black-eyed peas, water, 1 tsp of the thyme, and 1/2 tsp of oregano.
3. Once the peas are tender, add the reserved herbs and all remaining ingredients and simmer on low for at least 25 minutes to allow flavors to develop. If the soup is too thick, add up to two cups water or vegetable broth until it's the consistency of soup.
4. Serve with brown rice with additional hot sauce. (Garnishing with fresh oregano is optional.)

Collard Greens and White Bean Soup

Time: 1 hour 5 minutes / Servings: 6

Ingredients

- 1 large onion chopped
- 3-4 cloves garlic minced
- 1/2 pounds collards, kale, chard, or other greens tough ribs discarded and leaves chopped
- ribs celery chopped
- carrots sliced about 1/4-inch thick
- cups fat-free vegetable broth
- 1 tsp thyme
- 2 15-ounce cans white beans, drained
- 2-4 cups water or vegetable broth
- 1 1/2 tsp oregano
- 1 tsp thyme additional
- 1/4-1 tsp hot smoked paprika or chipotle chili powder adjust to your heat level
- 1/4 tsp red pepper flakes

- salt and freshly ground pepper to taste
- vegan Parmesan (optional)

Preparation Method

1. Heat an Instant Pot on Saute. Put the onion and cook, stirring, until onion is tender, adding water by the tablespoon to prevent sticking. Add the garlic and cook for another minute. Put the next 5 ingredients into the pot. Set manual setting for 5 minutes then quick release pressure.
2. Add two cups of water or broth, beans, and the remaining seasonings. Use saute electric pressure cooker at lowest temperature available for 20 minutes to allow flavors to mix.

Serve topped with vegan parmesan, if desired.

Green Moong Dal / Green Gram Lentil Soup

Time: 30 minutes / Servings: 4

Ingredients

- 1 cup green Moong dal or green gram lentils whole, rinsed
- 1 tbsp oil
- 1 Green chili chopped (optional)
- 1 tsp cumin seeds or jeera
- 1/2 tbsp garlic minced or paste
- 1/2 tbsp ginger minced or paste
- 2 tomato medium, chopped
- 1 onion medium, diced
- 1 tbsp lemon juice
- 3 cup water
- cilantro to garnish

Spices

- 1 tsp Garam masala
- 1 tsp coriander or Dhaniya powder
- 1/4 tsp Turmeric powder or Haldi
- 1 tsp Salt
- 1/2 tsp cayenne or red chili powder

Preparation Method

1. Set the instant pot on Saute and heat oil in it. Add the green chili and cumin seeds, and saute for 30 seconds.
2. Add onions, ginger, and garlic. Saute for 1 minute.
3. Add chopped tomato, spices and stir.
4. Add lentils and water. Stir well. Press CANCEL and close the instant pot lid with the vent in sealing position.
5. Press MANUAL or Pressure Cook mode for 15 minutes. When the instant pot beeps, let the pressure release naturally.
6. Open the lid and add lime juice and cilantro. Stir and green moong dal is ready to be served.

Thank You so much for reading this book!

I know you could have picked from many other books, but you chose this one. So big thanks for downloading this book and reading all way to the end.

If you enjoyed this book or received value from it, I'd like to ask you for a favor. Please take a few minutes to post an honest and heartfelt review on Amazon.com. Thanks so much!

Nelly Grant

Your Gift!

https://goo.gl/LCECyV

Manufactured by
Amazon.ca
Bolton, ON